YOU HAVE UNIVERSALITY.

POET AUTHENTICATOR & AUTHOR:
Ida Greenlee Cheeks

WEBSITE:
ifox.wordpress.com

E-MAIL:
ifoxproperties@aol.com

PHOTOGRAPHER:
Ida Greenlee Cheeks

CREDITS:
CLIP ART ICONS
BIBLICAL SCRIPTURES

ISBN: 9798648952553

IMPRINT: Independently Published

BOOK AVAILABILITY:
AMAZON Kindle Direct Publishing
www.amazon.com

YOU HAVE UNIVERSALITY.

~ CONTENTS ~

You Have Universality.

~ Prologue ~

Life curves this way sometimes to straighten our viewpoint of Grace to move on up a little higher… You Have Universality.

~ Ida Greenlee Cheeks

2017 BONUS Succinctly 2018 BE ON US
Like
The Sun…Shine…Rays
Healing
Growth
Changes
Life
Sustaining Elements
Essence and Presence
Celestial
Simplification
Definitively
Succinctly
Our Life
2017 BONUS
Within
2018 BE On Us
Without
Our
Interpretation has always been there here
Propagation has as Whom. What. When. Where. Why. How.
Always and Already been there
Because
It is a
2017 BONUS
Of life in our own
Time. Space. Place. Distant. Race. Grace.
Succinctly
If we understand it too to
2018 BE ON US
Everyday Now for a Way to View 365 Days
Sunrise to Meridian to Sunset
If we will let it be…

A windowed wintry landscape icicled snow-scape neighborhood
A Scope for Understanding Universally…
Glistening
People. Things. Places. Essence. Presence.
Healing
Growth
Changes
Wishing. Enduring. Believing. Receiving.
Listening
I leave with the Universe
Read. Decipher. Receive. Believe. We Will Remain Faithful!
2017 BONUS Succinctly 2018 BE ON US
Drawing Us like Water is from a bottomless pit of miry clay
Thoughts of degradation and deprivation…sinfulness and senselessness definientia
Causes. Words. Expressions. Characterizations.
We must want to be there
OH! But the
Sun…Shine…Rays
Power
Healing
Growth
Changes
Sustains
Lifting the prevailing
Sun Light Bright Celestially
Left in the Moment…Right there to here Terrestrially
See the implication is amplification and confirmation
Sounding
Like Street Consciousness too for Commonsensicalness finally sets in

Years of finalization for fruition arrived with a Cold Blast
Wintry Climate Acclimatization Dormancy for Normalcy
Sets in for recollection near to here to hear to bear what or who to witness…
2017 HAS DEPARTED 2018 HAS ARRIVED
Just like that, a Bomb Cyclone…a Bombogenesis Moment Warning Insanity
Learning Humane Rationality!
A song.
A snap the fingers.
A clap the hands.
A dance of the feet.
A wrap arms Around us.
A stance.
A blessed mind.
Abound
For
Universal Consciousness…
Genesis to Exodus
Intervals
For
Revelation
For
Transformation
For
Application
To
Assimilation
Time
2017 BONUS Succinctly 2018 BE ON US…
Compassionate Capacity
Health. Family. Friends. Associates. Adversaries Too.
Home. Clothing. Transportation. Wealth. Prosperity.
Wisdom to Understand the Differences
Of
Belief. Opinions. Behaviors. Principles. Needs. Wants.
Actions and Reactions
For
Abiding Faith. Hope. Joy. Love.
So, It Is To Be…AMEN!

ALIVE

The LORD
Has kept me
ALIVE…
I am Thankful.
Everyday
Everyway
Every Sway
Breezing
In the Winds of Life
Standing, Walking, Talking, Sensing My Surroundings
Gives me another chance
To Say on this Miraculous Journey of mine
The wonderment I see
Family
Friends
Oppositional Forces are a portion on the Table to Sit in the Chair then Stand
Digress, Emphasize, Stress, Relax not Break from the Point of Contention for
Coherence
Speak, Sing, Get Up, Lie Down
Sleep…Dream…Awakened I heard
Distinctly
The LORD
Has kept me
ALIVE…
I am Thankful.

Ask.
Their
Joy
Is
Insurmountable.
Dream
Voice
I hear
"And whatsoever you ask shall be given to you…"
I
Ask
For
Health
Wealth
Protection
For
Family
Friends
Universally
Sustained
Etc.

"And the LORD spoke unto Joshua, saying, Command the priests that bear the ark of the testimony that they come up out of Jordan. Joshua therefore commanded the priests, saying, Come you up out of Jordan. And it came to pass, when the priests that bare the ark of the covenant of the LORD were come up out of the midst of Jordan, and the soles of the priests' feet Were lifted up unto the dry land that the waters of Jordan returned unto their place, And flowed over all his banks, as they did before…That all the people of the earth might know the hand of the LORD, That it is mighty: That you might fear the LORD your God for ever." ~Joshua 4:15-18, 24

EVERY DAY
I have so many wonderful blended interesting questionable answerable ways
To say
I AM THANKFUL!
I think. I write text. I speak sing dance. I make mistakes. I make corrections.
I complete 30 or 31 Days…29 Days for Leap Year comes too sometimes
Then
EVERY DAY
365 Days a Year as 1.2.3…365 someway too today becomes
THANKSGIVING DAY
November 23, 2017
Is here to reminisce and think ahead…
I AM THANKFUL!
Continual Confirmation for Consideration
EVERY DAY
Past. Present. Future. Emotional Thoughts…
FEELINGS EMERGING
Camouflaged or Revealed

Immersions of Conversions and Dispersions
Family
Friends
Associates
Adversaries
Anyways
They will come then go to there becomes
EVERY DAY
All the sustenance magnified
Simplified and Said
Then
Exemplified instead then is Said

Everything is done this or that way in Life
Accordingly
The appearances for the reassurances
Visualized
Loneliness then Happiness of the Absence and Presence Happens
Come to Fruition
If
I continue to Believe
Anyways
I AM THANKFUL!
Come What May…
I Say
Preparation for Opportunities Surface
Autumn. Winter. Spring. Summer.
Differentiation
Is coming one way or the other way
KEEP ON STRIVING…
EVERY DAY

FRAGMENTAL
A Life State Being
Transcendental
Transformation
LIKE ROCKS
YOU HAVE UNIVERSALITY
Indicatively
Pathways
To See
To Be
Senses
To Do
THIS ABILITY WILLFULLY TO RECEIVE TO BELIEVE!
Spiritually
Soulfully
Physically
Emotionally
Intellectually
Culturally
Investigation
Descriptively
Holistically
Antiseptically
To For Being
FRAGMENTAL
A Life State Being
Awe-Inspiring
Adaptableness
LIKE ROCKS
YOU HAVE UNIVERSALITY
Indicatively
Pathways
To See
To Be
Senses
To Do
Consciously, Compassionately, Integrity, Purposefully, Passionately…
MIRACULOUSLY BEAUTIFUL WE ARE TO LIVE LIFE JOYOUSLY
PEACEABLY KINDLY COMPASSIONATELY LOVE PEOPLE!

FUNK OFF THE BACK
Bathe Oneself
Inclinations
Consequences…Circumstantial to Reality
Demonstrable
Doubtful
Accord
Discord
Afford
Expensive
Permit
Deforce
Happens
Find A Way to Understand
Why Believe Others and How We Do Not Believe Oneself…Get the
FUNK OFF THE BACK
Frontrunner
Straggler
Onboard
Not Onboard
Decisions…Intellectually and Emotionally
Cleansing Our Consciousness
Finally Sets the Mold…Told to Step In to Step Out…Get the
FUNK OFF THE BACK
Bathe Oneself
Intellectual and Emotional for Physical Inclinations…
Encouragement or Antagonistic
Comparatively…Innocence to Experience
Understanding Becomes the Best Education in Life…**PEACE!**

I was awakened by a voice…Annie or Mother or Mine
I think and reason…We are Mother and Sisters
Clarifying with Tonality
I heard in a moment of excitation…
"HELP ME!"
The wind blowing swiftly carrying the soundings
Wind. Windows. House.
Streets and Sanitation Workers. Garbage Trucks. Glass. Bottles.
Trains. Machines.
I heard distinctively.
I prayed again gratefully in that moment
For All the Matter and Energy in the Universe. People. Creatures. Everything.
Acknowledging, I am Thankful!
So, It Is To Be…
"His name shall be called
Wonderful,
Counselor,
The Mighty God,
The Everlasting Father,
The Prince of Peace."
Isaiah 9:6

I Have Written…Facets
Of My Life's Journey
Little Faces Surfaces in Memories
I in Life Live. Laugh. Love. Life to Care to Share with You…Will You, too?
Like Diamonds in the sky
Carats sparkling glistening listening sensing seemingly immeasurably
Like Dew Drops on the Earth
Percipitatively falling minutely scarcely intermittently abundantly Percipiently
Then to Now to Soon will be
Like Treasures in a Gift Box
Opening for Me the bows and ribbons and wrapping all taped
Like Memories flourish closely openly
Like peering through the Door a Way in Times
Presents in the Past Present Future Moment
Always there Anyways
I look at it…Come Is Goes
I Have Written…Facets
Of My Life's Journey
Aspects
Faces of Gemstones
Human. Zoologically. Anatomically. Physiologically. Psychologically.
Flora and Fauna Essence Presence Inspirationally
Family. Friends. Associates. Adversaries Inclusive not Exclusive
I in Life Live. Laugh. Love. Life to Care to Share with You…
Will You, too?
Wonderful Encapsulation Extrapolation Emancipation
Like Quilted Pieces
By
Great Grandmother Callie, Grandmother Arie, Aunt Allie, Mother Ruthie…
Life's Wisdom for Education in an Heirloom
Spiritual. Physical. Emotional. Cultural. Kindredship. Social.
So, It Is To Be
I Have Written…Facets
Of My Life's Journey
I hear to be awakened…
As the **Year 2017 Wane to Wax the Year 2018** to Shine Golden Age Rays
Prismatic Universally
"JONAH…Join Us!"
Sound…Like

There is going to be
**A Great Revival likens to Nineveh…Jonah in the belly of a
Whale?** Universally coming forth from the Dark to the Light
Like A Birthing Process...
Untruth details so Truth prevails…
Miracles Submerged now Revealed Blessings!
Sharing
Compassionately
Respectfully
Joyfully
Peacefully
Lovingly
Prosperity
Achievement
Substantiating Sustainability for Everyone Universally
Affirmation

I Saw the Prodigiousness in the Ordinariness
The Finale finally for myself
Mother…Grandmother
Life the way you all would like it too to be
Insightfully and Mindfully to Be Holistically
So, It Is To Be…
Spiritually. Physically. Emotionally. Culturally. Kindredship. Socially.
Love
Sharing
Humanely
Compassion
Wisdom
Knowledge
Understanding
The Concept of Healthiness and Abundance
Is not that
Hate
Does not exist but insist that I must resist the temptations that
Life that way is You All would not like it too to be
Greed. Ambition. Selfish Pleasure. Force.
Inhumane
Not Sharing
Lifeless
Scientific. Cultural. Outwardly Religious. Elegance.
Ignorance becomes Bliss…Miserable
I Saw the Prodigiousness in the Ordinariness
Life of Celebration in Continuation
I am Thankful too to Be…
Perceptively Recognizing the Years to Years Generational
1919 Conception to 1920 Reception to 1999 Transition Recollection
1933 Conception to 1934 Reception to 1970 Transition Recollection
1947 Conception to 1948 Reception to a Golden Age
1950 Conception to 1951 Reception to a Golden Age
1972 Conception to Reception to a Golden Age
2017
Disruptions for Dread. Tread the Air. Water. Land. Reassured for **Holistically**
Healing
Onward…Toward
2018

Futuristically
Shines Brightly on the Horizon
Faithful. Hopeful. Lovingly. Universally
For the People. Places. Things.
It is better too to **Tell the Truth not Lie…Pride goes before a Fall?**
I am Thankful to be Cognizant of the Fact that
Prayer. Provision. Purpose. Passion. Live Life. Laugh. Love. Family. Friends.
Associates. Adversaries Too.
I Saw the Prodigiousness in the Ordinariness

The Significance of a Toilet sitting on the Streets of Chicago, Illinois remembering a
Kosciusko, Mississippi View
**Laughing Out Loud Crying Humorously is Life Awareness Atoning Anointing
Ointment Blessing the Heart**
Realization. Stimulation. Elimination. Substantiation. Sustainability.
Transformation is in the process for progress.
Energization
Then
I Saw the Prodigiousness in the Ordinariness
As I sit in the glistening eastern Sun lights
Radiant Memories
Shine brightly for an Awakening
Holistically Healing
Spiritually. Physically. Emotionally. Culturally. Kindredship. Socially.
This Morning
12.28.2017
Slips away softly and briskly so whisperingly the touching sounds
On this wintry cold snowy visualization day to surface again another way
I say in this Time. Place. Space. Condition.
See and Hear to Recognize
Beauty in Being
Thoughtful proliferating for You 2

Mother…Grandmother
Liberation
Concentration
Disintegration
For
Unification
For
Rectification
Happens
For
The Best
Realization
Of
Life
The Universe will still come together again
As
Created
After
The Deep Surfacing
Of
Thoughts
Holistically Healing
I am Thankful!
I Saw the Prodigiousness in the Ordinariness

INCLUSION as In Clues I Own
Sharing In Conclusion
I visualize reading to write to speak to act to react on this Stage of Life
I have the Rights to Understand with Wisdom, Knowledge and Commonsense
The Mysteries of the Universe…Secrets unknown to known and untold to told
Engage mindfully to recognize on my Spiritual Journey
Expansion is of the essence and presence
I finally break the bonds of chain reactions to the unsolved
That which is solvable then resolve to see to do
What I need to relieve the pain and release the endorphins naturally
Withheld within the confine of genetic material and metabolic inheritance
Keeps unraveling like mosaic threads
Binding a Telomere-like shoelace replicates replenishing
The DNA-RNA Factors…46-paired Chromosomes

Like a Figure 8...…Intertwined Infinity
From the State of Creative Design Generational
INCLUSION as In Clues I Own
Sharing In Conclusion
I am going to be like Chicken Feet Signature Markings from Scratching
In the Prairie Snow
Precipitative…Then onto the Stormy Rain Drops…Embedding
In the Mississippi Pines Clay Dirt
Perceptive…Central Point of my Scripting…Receptive
Thoughts of Life as I have been to I am to I know to be…Being
Mindful. Respective. Civil. Respectful. Kind. Compassionate. Integrity.
Communicate. Fellowship. Faithful to Love Life Fulfillment
Introspectively not Exclusively but Inclusively
With Family. Friends. Associates. Adversaries Too. We are as Moments.
Seasonal Watershed Factors Change or Division
Flowingly drains like Lakes. Rivers. Oceans.

Isolationism
Plot
For An Universal Conversation
Cruelty to Humankind and Creatures and All Our Essence and Presence
Environmentally
On a larger scale
But
Commonsense. Tolerance. Compassion. Wisdom.
Sets in for Experiential Recognition
People Attempts for Dictating Life
Sneakingly not, even as a Squeaky Mouse naturally
But
As Family. Friends. Associates. Adversaries Too.
At least We Know How to Recognize
For Overpowering Other People's Will
For Slavery Conception is what happens
Actualizing
Abusive Relationships
Orally. Physically. Emotionally. Spiritually.
Bondages Happen
Centralizing Our Brains Capabilities
Strategic Politics Party Lines
Taking over…You can hear and visualize
The conversation invitation to listen to others on the same
Time. Place. Space. Distant. Near. Clear.
Thoughts scheming controlling taking over the Party…Lines
Characteristically For The
Isolationism
Plot
For An Universal Conversation
As Universal Consumption and Others Exclusion then Others
Become
Greed. Ambition. Selfish. Pleasure. Force.
Understandably…
I am Thankful for Our Choices…Decisions
Being in a State of No War Nor Hate but Love and Peace…Discerning
The
Isolationism
Plot

For An Universal Conversation
Definitively
I read for understanding explanatorily
How
Tolerance and Compassion is a Providential Requisite
Because Ominous States of Being Are…
Dictatorship
Separateness
Remoteness
Seclusion
Independence
Standoffishness
Pride
Xenophobia
Chauvinism
Sexism
Racial intolerance
Racism
Dislike
Of
Authentic Indigenous People.
Native People.
Natural Homegrown Born Citizens Bona Fide Colonized
Dislike of Foreigners
Belligerent Nationalism
Prejudice
Jingoism
Antipathy
Antagonism
Flag-Waving
Wrapping Yourself in the Flag
Become
Abreast Abreacting for Awareness
Psychologically
The Subliminal Messages
Eventually
Tension then Mention the Retention
Of
The Chicken Little Alarmist

Warning Imaginary Danger
Trauma Drama Mama Papa Children
Reliving Talking Walking Discerning for Realizing Releasing Living Healing
The
Isolationism
Plot
For An Universal Conversation
Haplessness to Hopelessness
Onward Toward
Hopefulness Intermingling Faithfulness
Fundamental for Health. Wealth. Being. Sustainable.
There will always be a Basking Conjecturing
Inside
Outside
Reality
Windowed
Sunrise. Meridian. Sunset.
Perseverant
Loving Living Life
Peaceably and Joyfully with a Purpose and Passion…
GRACE for ALL BEINGS!
So, It Is To Be…AMEN.

Life's Inquisitions
Call! Silence! Stall! Arise from the Fall!
Then there comes the Thrall?

People. Moral. Intellectual. Mental. Emotional. Physical…**CONVEY**
Forces of Domination is to be Overcome by Inspiration to get to Liberation…
HASTEN Clearance of the calcification for clarification
Deliverance of the indentation intention to clog the system of **OUR MIND**

Life's Inquisitions

Sending information to store or not store unwanted pellets of crystallization
Formation of intense, harsh and unfair this that these those other particles
Perhaps needed for Functionality…Reality gives us needed information
CLEARLY
Eating the right or wrong foods that can and cannot move
Through our Digestive Tract…**PROPERLY**
Breathing… Fresh Air or Fog. Smog. Fumes. Pollution. Ecosystem
Like particles that need a Filtration System…Flora and Fauna indicatives
Around for us to Breathe…**INCORRECTLY or CORRECTLY**
Clearance…Deliverance…Filterable for the Nose…Lungs overworked
Tiny particles moving through our Respiratory System…**INADEQUATELY**

However, in Time. Space. Opening for
Searching and Speaking and Actions Needed for Acquisitions through

Life's Inquisitions
Call! Silence! Stall! Arise from the Fall!
Then there comes the Thrall?

Qualms and Intuitions helps us with our Actions…Diseases…Healings…Feelings
Defying. Implying. Affirming. Coughing…Wheezing…Sputtering…Muttering…
HELP!
Can't we see the instigations then implications…**OVERCOME**

Life's Inquisitions

Old Wisdom…I Shall Have
Thoughts
Life
People
"You who have not sinned
(Have Not Trouble. Adversity. Misfortune),
Cast the first stone…"
At Other People in Their Glass House in a Storm…Chi
Shatters

Old Wisdom…I Shall Have
So, Let There Be
PEACE. JOY. COMPASSION. LOVE. In the UNIVERSE SHARING.
Let it begin with me
This 2017 Holiday Season
Approached is here now going near
The 2018 New Year
Is not far.
So, It Is To Be…Amen!
Old Wisdom…I Shall Have
Is a staple
Like food in the cupboard and refrigerator
For the Body needed
For the Soul to set my Spirit Free?
YES! Liberate To Understand
The Degree of intensity for propensity…
Criticism or felicitation digressing or focusing for conversation
Truth helps me too to mitigate not aggravate to concentrate to appreciate
That I Can Mind My Own Self-Righteous Business
Lest My own Glass House from Stones thrown in the Storm of Energy…Chi
From Other People Self-Righteous Business

Which Both
Shatters

Old Wisdom…I Shall Have
So, I do not **Cry** too much
From
Concealing. Appealing. Revealing.
It is just
HEAL…ING Water…Crying!
Denying. Defying. Clarifying. Recognizing.
Wondrous Outcomes
I began Trying Living Again Sustaining Power
Then
Thoughts
Life
People
I hear a loud thump
On the Family Room window,
A little startled
But recognize…
Bird, I guess searching for insects...
Bumped Its head but not dead instead just dread
A thread of energy...
Hear or Here…Hear-M! Here-M! Hear-M! Here-M!
Bass monotone melodic sounds
Not like the usual high pitched Birds I see and hear!
I look…No Bird…No Squirrel…
In sight for Insight
On the window ledge or grass or pavement outside inside
Danger, Harm, or Injury…
Confirmation
Safe, Secure, Sound All Around…
Inspiration

Old Wisdom…I Shall Have
Eventually has come
From
When I was younger
Childhood Developmental Stages
For
Purposeful Journeys
Wilderness to Exodus to a Place of Arrival Needed I surmise
The Lonely Times were not Profound in my Vocabulary nor Emotions nor
Thoughts
Did not resonate
But Now
I am more Golden Aged
I see to revisit and omit and add and admit are needed
Golden Rays of Sunshine Chi…Energy of Life…Breath to Breathe
The Essence and Presence for my Body. Soul. Spirit.
Fortitude

Then to Now…
Sharing Standing Sitting Relaxing to Orchestrate the Nutrients
I concentrate to mediate to alleviate the aches and pains for relief and joy
From
Clutter. Sputter. Mutter. Clatter. Splatter. Gossip. Falsehoods. Slanderous. Libelous.
To
Overcome
For
Truth
Proliferate
And
Matters
In
Our Universal
Thoughts
Life
People
Old Wisdom…I Shall Have

Rejection or Acceptance
Is Sometimes
Dejection to a Behavior
Adjacent Conceptually Becomes
Rejection or Acceptance
Is to be Viewed as an Exception to the Rule
Are Most of the Times?
How We Look at a Situation
Happiness to a Behavior
Obscure
Attitude
Accusation or Affirmation
Trial
Tribulation or Comfort becomes a Probability
Adjudication
Trivial or Crucial as Truth or Untruth
Therefore, is always a Cause and Effect in Life to Live?
Purposefully or Aimlessly
There are Consequences and Solutions in the Mind…A Conscious Thing
Rejection or Acceptance
Realization is to tidy up the Rough Stuff to get to the Smooth Stuff
Enclosed…Concealed to be Disclosed
Do not forget the sealed box that becomes opened to pickup the Pieces to the
Puzzle
Unfound then Found Connecting for Completion
Challenges to Routines
Perplexities to Simplicities
Comprehensibly to Overcome to Be Calm to Live
Not Detrimentally but Beneficially
Spiritually. Physically. Emotionally. Culturally. Kindredship. Socially.

Request…Requiem or Commemoration
Order
Tribute
Honor
Remembrance
Service
For
Life to Live then a significant Being is here then gone
Everlasting
Memories
Shared
Covert to Overt then Divert to Release and Focus…Is a way of Life?
We all must travel one way or the other one-day…Sooner than Later
Will be a Time. Space. Place. Grace.

Reckoning
Restrain then Release the Negative Energization within Us is Amongst Us…
Rumormongers. Retaliations. Recurrences. Repercussions.
Refutation for Confirmation becomes an Understanding
State of Disturbances for the Mind
Then Who. What. When. Where. Why. How.

Beckoning
The Calm After The Storm
Truth-Seekers and Torchbearers.
Refuge. Relax. Rest. Rejuvenate. Recreation. Readjust. Reformative.

Respite
Belief for Relief of Positive Energization Within Us Surrounds Us…
State of Peace for the Mind
Acknowledgement

Balances

Our Life

Immortalization happens for some more than others to live on as do…
Art. Music. Painting. Poetry. Novel. Movie. Fact or Fiction.
Genres. Etc. etc. etc.
Request…Requiem or Commemoration
Transformation
Like 2017 ends to begin 2018 and years to come never ends
Realization sets in to Live and Let Live
Tracks in Time are Here to There
To see as Whom. What. Why. Where. When. How.
It seems until one day or another day begins the Rounds of Life it appears
Gone are the thoughts on this end…
Boundaries of Life it appears until another phase sets in eventually
Life to Live then a significant Being is here then gone
Such As Is Still Will Be Justifingly
Understanding Our Universal Walls and Bridges and Flora and Fauna after
Questions and Answers
Vanishing
Like a mist of watered snowflakes is as a breath away!

Sensitivity for Sensibility…Transforming
Starts with Home Training through Teaching and Learning Civility…
Raised therefore Shaped
Spiritually. Physically. Emotionally. Culturally. Kindredship. Socially.
The Rise of a Nation…
Home to the World Intermingling Everyone and Everything
I see. I hear. I feel. I sense. I taste. I touch.
The Atmosphere's Climatic Zone

Simply: tropical zone near the equator, two subtropical and two temperate zones, one boreal zone in the northern hemisphere, and the two polar ice caps…**weather**, temperature, environment, microclimate, macroclimate, climatic zone, atmosphere, **situation**, ambiance, surroundings, environment, conditions, feeling, mood, **sense**

Family. Friends. Associates. Foes.
Food. Water. Health. Homes. Clothing. Transportation. $. Words. Actions.
Bitterness or Sweetness…Conclusively needs some
Sensitivity for Sensibility…Transforming
Starts with Home Training through Teaching and Learning Civility…
Raised therefore Shaped
Air. Land. Water.
The Rise of a Nation…
Home to the World Intermingling Everyone and Everything
Fallen through not recognizing our ignorance to the facts willfully
Uplifted by acknowledgment through the winds beneath our wings
Soaring higher cognizant to the facts willfully
Grace Abounds…Being Humane One towards Another…Generosity of Spirit
Simply: Capacity to Tolerate. Accommodate. Forgive.
Ourselves 1st then Others in Order
Sensitivity for Sensibility…Transforming
So, It Is To Be…Seen. Experienced. or Believed. Received.

Conceptualizing: "Fix these words of mine in your hearts and minds; tie them as symbols on your hands and bind them on your foreheads. Teach them to your children, talking about them when you sit at home and when you walk along the road, when you lie down and when you get up. And you shall write them upon the door posts of your house, and upon your gates…Behold, I set before you this day a blessing and a curse; A blessing, if you obey the commandments of the LORD your God, which I command you this day: And a curse, if you will not obey the commandments of the LORD your God, but turn aside out of the way which I command you this day, to do after other gods, which you have not known." ~Deuteronomy 11:18-20; 26-27

Smile…Again!
Sometimes
Life
Have fears to overcome
But
Smile…Again!
Before
The cheers of Life come to make
Life Free
Smile…Again!
Then
So
I will write the pain for gain away to stay in this Life
Makes me
Happy
Again
This day
I say
Sway on Baby Girl
Woman
I am to Be Now…
Mother and Grandmother and Now My Baby Arthur 11.20.2019 are gone
Now
A Long, Long Time Ago
It appears to be to me
Preordained
But
As I rewrite this Script of Memories
It is in The Holy Spirit's Hands and Will and Power too to Be…
Not Mine but in Time
I Understand
Although
I Yearn…I Learn…I am Forlorn it appears too to forward to Thoughts Loving
Anyways
Remembrances
Proliferate until I began to
Smile…Again!
Awakened
From

That

Which

I read in my dreams

Romans 8:8 then verse 8:2

I read now to read now and now I write…

"So then they that are in the flesh (carnal)

Cannot please God."

Then

"For the law

Of the Spirit

Of life

In

Christ Jesus

Has made me free

From

The law of sin (trouble, adversity and misfortune)

And

Death (Sleep)."

The Redemptive Price now is The Redemptive Power…

The Mystery

Suffering Glory...Rest

I heard. I touched. I saw. I sense. I Believe. I Receive.

Inspirationally

So, It Is To Be!

AMEN.

Smile…Again!

STATE of BEING

Action
Reaction
Asleep
Awakened
Cognizant of the Fact concentrate

Marching Onward
In Life

Atypical sometimes but Always Attuned…Symbolize

WORDS of INSPIRATION

The message to consume daily to resume…
Hesitant…Non-defeatist…Resistant…Resilient…

Marching Onward
I must recognize

To be apprise of the insinuation is for recognition for realization
Choices I choose to wisely be in as a

STATE of BEING

Peripherally to eye all the corners of life
To turn onto into the realm participation should be
Civility
For myself and others and energy I place in the Universal Synchronicity
That is All I Know….
Thoughts proliferate
Action
Reaction
Asleep
Awakened
Cognizant of the facts concentrate Marching Onward in Life
Atypical sometimes but Always Attuned…Symbolize

WORDS of INSPIRATION

Truths or Lies submerge to emerge as the consequences of actions…reactions
Talking
Walking
Living as the Proof in a

STATE of BEING

Clearly I hear the voice speaking to me I write as I read about even now…

"You all right with this?"

I recall recapturing a Time of Capitulation
But

Perseverance is the Steadfastness of Grace in a
STATE of BEING
Assuredly I write from I read in its entirety
Psalm 35:1-28
To share

WORDS of INSPIRATION
Universally for Comforting…
Myself. Family. Friends. Associates. Adversaries.
Observation of All Nature
11: False witnesses did rise up; they laid to my charge things that I knew not.
12: They rewarded me evil for good to the spoiling of my soul.
13: But as for me, when they were sick, my clothing was sackcloth: I humbled my soul with fasting; I prayed with head bowed on my bosom.
14: As though I grieved for my friend or my brother and sister, I went about as one who laments his mother.
15: But at my stumbling, they gathered in glee. They gathered together against me; cripples whom I knew not slandered me without ceasing;
16: They impiously mocked more and more, gnashing at me with their teeth.
17: How long, O LORD, will you look on? Rescue me from their ravages, my life from the lions!
18: Then I will thank YOU in the great congregation; in the mighty throng, I will praise YOU.
20: For they do not speak peace, but against those who are quiet in the land they conceive words of deceit.
21: They open wide their mouths against me; they say, "Aha, Aha! Our eyes have seen it!"
22: YOU have seen, O LORD, be not silent! O LORD, be not from me!
25: Let they not say to themselves, "Aha, we have our heart's desire!" Let them not say, "We have swallowed him up."
27: Let those who desire my vindication shout for joy and be glad, and say evermore, "Great is the LORD, who delights in the welfare of his servant!"
28: Then my tongue shall tell of YOUR righteousness and of YOUR praise all the daylong…

WORDS of INSPIRATION
Walking and Talking
Action. Reaction. Asleep. Awakened. Cognizant.
STATE of BEING

STORY LINES
For the Story Board Being. Creative. Believing. Receiving
The Reason for the Season
Waiting through the Solstices and Equinoxes Departs…Arrives
12.25.2017
Winter Intermittent Twilight. Spring Renewal. Summer Golden Age. Autumn
Vigorous Recurrence.
Precipitation Comes…Goes Anticipation…Returns Faith
Visualizing
Listening
Learning
Teaching
Reaching
Practicing
Guiding
Sharing
Inspiration
Understanding
Oneself…Others…Universally
Family. Friends. Associates. Adversaries.
Inclusively not Exclusivity
Health. Home. Food. Safe and Secure. Wealth. Clothes. Transportation.
Are
STORY LINES
For the Story Board Being. Creative. Believing. Receiving
I am Thankful for Life to get in Sync
The Link to Family and Friends in Accordance not Avoidance
Of our essence and presence of All Nature
Live immersed in sight for what is right not for erroneous doctrine
Laugh along the way alone then accompanied
Love immensely breathtakingly sensing
Life perpetuity is possible too
Resurrected from Dormancy
Entrenched with Grateful Thoughts
Following not darkness
But have **The Light of Life**
Miraculously this Day and Everyday and Noonday and Evening and Night
Onward Toward a New Horizon…Possible…**Sunrises to Sunsets**
With interspersed scenery vanishing appearing

The Twinkling of an Eye…
Moon, Trees, House, Geese in Flight…Sky Line
Viewing Closely the Sight Intermingled
STORY LINES
For The Story Board Being. Creative. Believing. Receiving
"THE WAY SHOWER"
This Christmas Day. Evening. Night.
Shadows
I hear. I see. I sense. The Curtain Call of the Sunset nearby as the Geese
Sounding Stillness in Awe Appreciation
Orchestrating Synchronizing in the Opening Curtain
Is a Sunrise nearby…
Picturesque
Up Above My Head…
Listening attentively is Life Below My Feet…
Also inconspicuous but obvious to immerse
Faith. Hope. Love. Life. Live.
Our Experiences
In the Right Season is Every Season
Of the Year for the Reason
Is to Continue…Change
For the Betterment for Humankind
And
All Creation…Universally!

SUMMER DAYS
Are coming
I will write about
In God's Will To Be…Prayerfully I Say Meditatively
MISSISSIPPI
When I arrive to be too, I am already happy for the thought.
I ought to just hug myself and conscientiously
The Battles of Life have already been fought
For Family. Friends. Associates. Adversaries too
CHICAGO, ILLINOIS NOSTALGIA on the STREETS of TIME

To Live. Laugh. Love. Life with Purpose and Passion Enthusiastically

I shall in appreciation
Without any reservation or verbalization of naught
But
Significance for association is
The Moral. Social. Value. Justifiable.
SUMMER DAYS
Are coming
I have already sought the route to take initially
Comes in a projective respective order

AUTUMN. WINTER. SPRING.
Caught up
In the Sightline of Artistic Webbing Unambiguously Being
I will speak futuristically into existence
The Time
Which shall come ultimately
In God's Will To Be…
Prayerfully
I Say
Meditatively
MISSISSIPPI

Where I Come From…Conversation
Initiation for Consideration
Talk the Talk and Walk the Walk to Sense the Universality You Have.
Sensibly becomes Interrogation for Life
Implication
Fact from Fiction is the realization
Reservation to Go…On to Come…Back to How Life really is
Where I Come From…Conversation
Answers all the gibberish slipperiest naughtiest haughtiest
Caught sensibly to the misrepresentation
A continuation comes to me in my mind my own business scenario
As you mind your own business
Where I Come From…Conversation
Initiation for Modification from Mortification to Fortification
For Life has its own Confusion…Humiliation and Resolution…Strengthening
Confirmation to clear myself from Indignation to an Implication
Doing Wrong to understand how Doing Right is Paramount
Where I Come From…Conversation
Recollection for Instantiation is needed
On my Journey as a Safety Net for Humanness
People. Health. Home. Places. Wealth. Transportation. Security.
Respect. Integrity. Dignity.
Crooked…Hope it's a Shepherd's Hook for guidance
Slick…Become Your Own Trick
To intellectualizing and emotionalizing for stabilizing
Fake…Make the bed hard of soft or just right
Straight…Narrow Paths
Are already and always there for Normalcy
Eventually
You tell…I can tell…They can tell
Lies or Truth had better Get it from wrong to right
Might surface one day sight someway somebody will stay to say
Testimonial Shamefully or Uplifting to surmise to surprise to undeniably
OOPS!
There it comes another way anyway
That's Life…It just be and is that way
In an ordinary Day. Midday. Evening. Night. Moonlit or Cloudy surfaces
Shade to Fade to Close to Ajar to Open a Sunlit Window to Door to House
An Old to New to Set Out to Settled In

Where I Come From…Conversation
Recollection Time Visualization
Recognition of Life Destination and Provision for Natural Phenomena and Living
Lie down rest then Rise up Rejuvenation to see the way
Of how Life should be…
Can't see but maybe Need to see
Realization sets the mold and told to scold
Or
Extol unfold the concealed sought to sold or bought in to brought out
Spiritual. Physical. Emotional. Cultural. Kindredship. Social.
Words to Speak for Action to a Reaction.
Revelation to Admission.
Application from Dormancy towards Transformation.
Receptiveness towards Assimilation.
A Vivifying Mode of Life is worth Living
Where I Come From…Conversation

YOU HAVE…
ETHOS
Ethnologically
Shows Us
Comparatively
Life Moments of Rhythm
Melancholy. Tear Shed. Crying. Anguish.
Through Seasonal Cloudy White Grey Black, Orange Golden Sky Blue
Precipitately Appears a Ray of Sunshine Prismatic Rainbow of Comfort
Joy. Smiles. Laughter. Content.
Life Moments of Rhythm
Watershed
Relapse
Dishearten One Another
Embolden One Another
Civility
Rudeness
In Spite of All the Circumstances
We Share…
Fundamental Traits
YOU HAVE…
A Backup for Definitiveness…
ETHOS
Ethnologically
Life Moments of Rhythm
Social. Perspective. Time. Expressions. Attitudes. Habits.
Philosophy. Beliefs. Character. Morals. Principles.
YOU HAVE…
Distinctive **(+/-)** Qualities
ETHOS
Wisely Chosen…Determinants

You Have Universality.
~ Epilogue ~

INSPIRATION:
<u>Old Testament</u>
JOSHUA 4:15-18, 24
PSALMS 35:1-28
PROVERBS 3:1-7
ISAIAH 9:6
<u>New Testament</u>
ROMANS 8:1-38
ACTS 7:44-59
EPHESIANS 4:4-7

"Everyone Has Their Own Path.

Walk Yours With Integrity And Wish All Others
PEACE
On Their Journey."
~ UNKNOWN ~